FINISHING LINE PRESS

www.finishinglinepress.com

Green River Road

poems by

Michael Levell

Finishing Line Press
Georgetown, Kentucky

Green River Road

For Ryan Charles Chighizola

ACKNOWLEDGMENTS

"Favor" was originally published in issue 44, August 2017, of *birdy.*
magazine.

I would like to thank my mom for the cover photo and Erin Fishburn for
the author's photo. I would also like to thank my friends and family for their
encouragement and support and all the authors living and dead who have
inspired and helped give voice to these poems.

Publisher: Leah Maines
Editor: Christen Kincaid
Cover Art: Pat Levell
Author Photo: Erin M. Fishburn
Cover Design: Leah Huete

Printed in the USA on acid-free paper.
Order online: www.finishinglinepress.com
         also available on amazon.com

Author inquiries and mail orders:
Finishing Line Press
P. O. Box 1626
Georgetown, Kentucky 40324
U. S. A.

Table of Contents

About a Photograph

baked to a single loaf
up along castled streets

over last Sunday's sudden rain
thrown into the west

to move more deeply through
its aqueous sunset

in among seeding thistles
silver purples

exact gratitudes
breads of sunlight

on great platters of laughter
dissolved unsolved

Perchance

the instance
of immortal

iridescent
fruitage

discards
circumstance

as an entity
its advanced

approach
only accepts

Giant Nests over the Black City

Dreaming that her belly was an elephant heart plum and that chokecherries were embedded in her lower guilt, she thought of justice, loved him, and did not go inside. The day before the dead maple burned, they formed an equilateral triangle. The youngish man, a trifle overweight, too anxious for his age, completed his circuit and stood by the door, ashamed as usual. An orange ruled the world.

At first, she felt like a girl band in trouble, every hit a voice in her head lowering her lip made of black marble, black and clean; yet today, from the spyglasses up in the old tree, the marble in the middle of her desert was hundreds of miles away. It was back in her room, with her gone for pizza, that he initially found himself alone and prying, looking around admiring her tastes, wondering whether to bring her flowers.

They stayed restless, read in the newspaper a few decades later how at that time crime was at an all-time low, but he still wouldn't go to the old wooden hotel because it was quiet except for the throb of the waves. All crockery and repertory bunk, he made his name as a professional thief of handbags until he found himself listening to an uninterrupted hour of chatty remarks about her panorama.

Then suddenly, she appeared hazy, halfway focused, a murmur passed the docks by the gates of the Black City where wiry boys hoist gunnysacks and shout to each other. She just foundered and foundered, saying exactly what their parents would have if they were moody and bored with silver stars. She would bound for the next new crescent and ride it through the night where at least she wouldn't have to hear his questions. "Did you not fear for your mother?" The girl was young when she did, lived the green exterior disguises a woman uses to know herself somewhere between childhood and the main reason he dragged her into the bright beach house to the albatross that killed their parents.

Really, there's not much to tell. Squawks made them. His father had not meant to abuse them, had not meant to since 1927, but divers searching for drowned children and drowned mothers swear they've seen their evidence like cats in a prison recreation hall. Falling from favor or grace, from some high artifice, down they dropped like discredited predicates through what was then called a poor boy and girl left on their small shelf next to a half-finished cup of do not divide or die.

Years after the story's death caught both of them off guard, their differences grew like drunk lightning, their arms reaching out across the bed like a sky full of clear buttons, its air surveyed for progress. Erosion was the greatest threat to the stability of how their parents got caught in that car engine and blew up.

Seduced by yesterday, they looked up each other's looks, and up further into the big tree out front to see these gigantic nests they left behind the size of black sofas, but in a frayed wool sweater, with sword splitting consequences, she undermined his ability to cope with what a bullet could do.

One catastrophe after another her mother said meaning her. She drank single malt out on the porch and leaned toward the ocean. She said to him, "Before you go, light a cigarette under the old red maple in the front yard, under this hunter's moon, and take a last look, so you won't have to change."

In Fragments toward Oblivion

virtue owns a more eternal foe
since crawling hope's twin

destinies weave graves from
a glorious phantom force

a rock built refuge standing old
mad blind dead as a lone star

whose light shines frail winter's
midnight roar upon a platinum

pedestal where these words appear
unheeding to many an old wrinkled

command to look on mighty
despair who neither sees nor feels

nor knows but to leech a fainting
cling to one who has lifted thee

The Strange World of Adults

back when I was more
of a rube some things

didn't have to make sense
outside of their theory

of finding a better balance
among I told you so

turned in thanks from
a readymade world

around which I allowed
myself to deserve

and to think
most all of this to be real

That's Why

because some
are not ready

to accept one
can generate

a next correct
based on what

is needed
to get this far

Ruts

distance at speed
how bodily it travels

making crooked the
wise animal's state

overcome by the sun
set so silently upon

winded birds along
a wire's extension

what shining tracks
breezes needle down

the old scarred road
of endless foreground

Poem

before thoughts had words
or uncounted generations

moved magical and smart
notices further back tossed

materials granted this world
each person's incomparable

legend of an occupied mind
the fear and fear and fear

of all our lives absorbed to
a silent rusty pink hydrangea

lying on a dead young mother
or an empty old broke ship

the world will end like a poem
that could have been our own

Beast of O

the ideal of roses stands
high along our avenue

scattered among a future's
incredibly rare balm

caught behind your eyes'
unchanging calm a burnt

white lullaby whose chosen
song blasts many endarkened

centuries upon a common
impressionistic alas

William Thomas

1.
two days before Thanksgiving
a man flagged me down from the street
he pointed to my hat
said he loved it
said it reminded him of back in Seattle when he just turned 30
a long time ago
when he was working for a laundry
and got himself a green fedora
with a red stripe around it
it was one of his favorite things he ever had
I shook his hand of dirty bloated hard sausages
and wiped my eye as he talked about being alone
I gave him three bus tickets
in lieu of cash for keeping warm
I was Michael (also his brother's name
whose middle name was James also my father's name)
he was William (my godfather's name)
and when he was 17 he went down to Mexico
with his friends
said he blew everything and fucked everything
if I knew what he meant

2.
two days after Thanksgiving
I saw William Thomas again
Christopher he yelled to me
Michael I replied to his embarrassment
we talked about my green fedora
he asked me where I lived and if I had a wife
and since I didn't he could hook me up
with some chick named Pixie he called her that
because she had a short haircut and came just up to here
he said she was beautiful and asked if he could kiss her
she said no and she said she was glad that he asked first

she was 28 instead of his assumed 21 and they talked and talked
he said his wife was somewhere else
and everyone was against him his daughters even his son
said his wife forgot to renew the lease
and a sheriff who was tall and a little deputy
gave him 24 hours to leave the property
asked have you ever woken up to a sheriff pounding at your door
pointing to his leg said his wife was recovering in some home
somewhere
and didn't want him around
and hell yeah it's tough I live everywhere now
then he asked me how I'd been
told him that I was recovering from the flu
to which he responded
maybe that's where I got it from

Elegy

dirt lots family pictures catfish
down deep in the cold mud

I serpentine abandoned shopping
center pillars beneath headphones

in the middle of a way out there
are no trails no front porch couches

just a sky so high with attention
vagabond fishermen forget

by the old pond our love follows
not knowing how to muck out

a town free of famous people
lungs and guts bury this farmland

invisible struggles break through the
ferocious nature of misunderstood

suns trying so hard to escape
surprised deer on the front lawn

all the earth's heroes in return
dusty eyes before a great storm front

Christmas Letter to a Dead Friend

choices continue who I am
interdependency hangs human

and thinks of you the only
imposition to this damn cold

morning doesn't know either
what'll happen next or how long

the eagers of perfection will crack
silly upon their own securities

by the way it snowed pretty hard last
night so thanks for the Tennessee

sippin' cider and the lights oh the
lights how I wish you could see them

Well Shit Fire

part emulating what I admire
part until we meet blinded

by languages' event transported
ages unedit like a mountain

flatly left in the dark I catch
the neurotic intoxication of

your milk weed find out without
approval personal pronouns

can change until finally my bed
is warm and I don't wanna

give up what I learned from the
grip of a god the cold of a day

or entering a forest at night

I Think It was a Plain Old Robin

blanket up to chin
monsters strung out

on the sudden angular
fist of total now

had another dream
the knocking step

a bird blinded for
slandering sentries

with some archaic
feeling words possess

a piece of electricity
a shadow freed

5 Poorly Translated Love Poems

1.

little birds sing
of stawberry blossoms
in the deep desert

gentle perennial showers
thicken creeks
in the growing breeze

the perfume of various
social trees plunder
the trembling eye

its sapphire blush
soon at a stunning rush

2.

at first
everyone is

a little scared
to pop their danger

they awaken
they push off

they are very much
mistaken

3.

a greater life passes the brighter
the light encourages its own delight
but old winds shape and lift and
change perpetual dreams reveal the
wildness over the waters revive
more than a heart can raise or ruin
break or illuminate until eyes
barely know their sharp lights
winter capes command chance or
maybe midnight to replace silences
off the darkness without taking on
more than what flourishes

4.

if the limits
of love

overcome
thy view

do not be
surprised

5.

simply put you
remove all ideas
of covering up
anything further

After the Late Show

warm room
cold night loud
morning stairs

where I never was
anyone else who
didn't do it and was

not also done to
so marvelously so
cold out there still

Guttered

dented breath
porcelain ear

down here

without light
or allowance

willful
magnanimous
and cruel

At a Loss

angry private
wings of self

conclusion
beat mad

marooned
in strange

communion
to inexorably

remove any
superfluous

limp flutter
of faint dignity

Lion

to begin the lion all bulk and missing for years
its huge face no chapel no hill no little gate
leading to the forest only lion about to speak of

a place where images reside like something sacred
in something missing my mouth changes people
cupcakes elves aliens or perhaps a favorite celebrity

these have little to do with me I'm full of them as much
as they are full of cupcakes elves aliens and perhaps
a favorite celebrity they live through my roar my

magnificent teeth the natural disaster of my presence
I used to believe my job was to help save people
from being lions but now I see the lion's coat its

open mouth my invitation to step upon its pillowish
pink tongue then oh so dark proscenium
the inseparable return that knows no contest

when inside a lion only transformation to wake to
breathe so deeply through shivering morning's choice

In Effect

the mediation of the other
is illuminated by

the gaze raised
toward the last grasp

the mediation of the other
is illuminated by

Venom in Rust

induced by the powerful
seclusion felt by a hand

lifted from a blunt stone
the fable's musk grips like

a tunneling mosaic unaware
of figures in raw bloom

inimitable and resolute its
mythic quarry bends at

the waist like a rose plum
wrenched from its socket

~~Did You Ever Find My Hand in Yours; Have You Checked Yet?~~
Favor

one thing placed to the next
makes this world appear so real
when left behind

an apparition
fit so snuggly in its explanation

only part topography of the
fortresses we command upon
distant hills

as I stroll through
the generative hand somehow

larger within yours
if found
please return to heaven

Notes

"5 Poorly Translated Love Poems" come from 5 poems on an open domain poetry website where each poem selected was put through Google translator and then edited or used as original material.

"About a Photograph" borrows lines from Denise Levertov for original material.

"At a Loss" uses lines from Jack London's *The Call of the Wild, White Fang & To Build a Fire,* Modern Library 100 Best Novels edition as original material.

"Beast of O" borrows lines from each poem from: http://www.poetryintranslation.com/PITBR/French/Mallarme.htm#anchorToc223495085 then put into an online translator: https://www.bing.com/search?q=free%20translator%20&qs=n&form=QBRE&pq=free%20translator%20&sc=8-16&sp=1&sk=&cvid=0D52C8A326624F8BABD6D8DFB5FEF4E3 Translated from English to French then back to English on Google translator then used as original material.

"Elegy" is after Frank O'Hara's "Elegy".

"Giant Nests over the Black City" borrows first lines in reverse order from *Flash Fiction Forward,* edited by James Thomas & Robert Shapard, Norton, 2006, as original material.

"In Effect" uses Lines from *In Praise of Love* by Alain Badiou with Nicholas Truong as original material.

"In Fragments toward Oblivion" borrows lines from http://www.sonnets.org/shelley.htm#200 for original material.

"I Think It was a Plain Old Robin" uses Anne Carson's *Autobiography of Red* as original material.

"Lion" is from a prompt by and uses "cupcakes elves aliens and perhaps a favorite celebrity" from "the Seven of Muses," a poetry tarot card from the twosylvias press app.

"Perchance" borrows lines from *Arcana of Spirituality* for original material.

"Ruts" borrows lines from Larry Eigner's *The World and Its Streets, Places* as original material.

"The Strange World of Adults" borrows lines from Lisa Jarnot's *A Princess Magic Presto Spell* for original material.

"Venom in Rust" uses Barbara Guest's *Defensive Rapture* as original material.

Original Material as mentioned above uses the works mentioned as a word bank which is sometimes kept, sometimes edited and sometimes has other notebook materials added to it in the making of the poem.

Michael Levell was born and raised in Evansville, Indiana where he began his love of poetry. He spent a short amount of time in Tulsa, Oklahoma where he was the host of several poetry venues including the Gypsy Coffee House open mic nights. He received his MFA in Writing and Poetics from Jack Kerouac's College of Disembodied Poetics at Naropa University. His work has appeared in *Bombay Gin, madeupmovement. com, shampoopoetry.com, the Found Poetry Review,* and *birdy.* among other journals. He lives in Denver, Colorado and teaches Composition, Literature and Creative Writing at the Community College of Aurora in Aurora, Colorado. This is his first chapbook.